Collins.

Signed limited
Edition of 1400 copies

each, slipcase
£15·0

Fifteen

(72120)

(A)

PICTURES ON GLASS

FRONTISPIECE (overleaf): CORINTHIAN WOOD

PICTURES ON GLASS

engraved by

LAURENCE WHISTLER

1972

THE CUPID PRESS

Of this book

fourteen hundred copies have been printed
for the Cupid Press, Barham Manor, Ipswich, Suffolk,
of which four hundred copies have been reserved for
subscribers in the United States of America.
The text and illustrations have been printed
by the Westerham Press, of Westerham, Kent,
and the blocks have been engraved by
the Grout Engraving Company, of Bromley.
The binding is by W. & J. Mackay
of Lordswood, Chatham, Kent.

This is number

673

Laurence Whistler

ISBN 0 903575 00 0
© Laurence Whistler 1972
Printed and bound in Great Britain

For Hugh and Vera Dawson

WITH LOVE AND GRATITUDE

Acknowledgement

THE WORKS SHOWN are a selection of those engraved during fourteen years: between 1959 and 1972. I thank Her Majesty The Queen for gracious permission to illustrate one work; and I am grateful to the owners of other engravings, as named in the notes.

Nearly all the photographs were taken for me by Anthony Osborn (Nos 1– 29), followed by Graham Herbert.

LW

Little Place, Lyme Regis, Dorset

Introduction

IT IS BEST to begin by describing how most of the pictures in this book were made. They were drawn on the bowl of a glass with a steel point held in a tool like a pencil, no acid and no mechanical process coming into it, except that here and there, though very seldom, the same kind of point was held in a slow-revolving drill.* The picture is built up mainly of extremely small dots put on at speed by a vibrating hand, and with a pressure perhaps less than that of a pencil on paper, a technique that would be called stippling if the dots did not merge into longer marks and lines, and sometimes into areas scratched or abraded all over, to achieve maximum whiteness. That is to say, whiteness will result when the glass is placed in a good light, falling from behind, against a background that is black or at least shadowy. For against a white sky or a white wall there is no contrast, the boldest engraving hardly tells, and the most delicate becomes invisible. It is by contrast that the picture comes to view, as the unengraved areas disappear into darkness. As for light, nothing equals the sun, which brings everything to life; and, failing direct sunlight on the bowl, artificial light is required. Consequently in glass a picture is elusive, and more subservient to setting than in any other medium. By way of compensation, when the setting is good the scene will appear to hang in mid-air as if the light were within it rather than against it, or as if it were composed of the light.

My aim is to make glass a pictorial medium like canvas or paper. Why, then, it may be asked, not use it, like canvas or paper, in the flat – no less for small-scale work than for large-scale windows or panels? The answer is two-fold.

Available flat glass is very hard, and therefore crude to engrave: it blunts a point very quickly and tends to splinter under it. This does not matter when the scale is enlarged and bold effects are required, but for delicate effects one needs soft glass, which means glass with plenty of lead in it; and lead glass is only made by firms that blow it into circular shapes. That is why the panels in 'A Seasons Centrepiece' (Plates 33 to 35), 'The Festival' (Plates 38 and 39), and 'From Castle to Airport' (Plate 54), are not flat but slightly dish-shaped. They were cut from the largest sphere that could be blown.

Then, even if flat glass were available, one would not want to abandon the

*For a few designs reproduced, and especially for those on a larger scale, on windows and panels, this hand-engraving was supplemented by other techniques mentioned in the Notes on the Plates.

[7]

curved surface of a bowl for small-scale work. The picture comes to no arbitrary stop on each side like the edge of a frame: fading out, it can seem to go on indefinitely. If it is drawn on the far side, in reverse, in the manner that I call back-engraving, to be looked at across the bowl from in front, the viewer may have some illusion of being inside the secret world of the scene; and illusory effects are appropriate to glass, as I hope to show later on.

But a bowl by itself will be fingered, and finger-marks will dim the engraving. It needs to be raised on a stem. Then a stem needs a foot to stand on. So we arrive, pragmatically, at a required general form, and find it to be familiar, the form of a goblet or drinking-glass. Only, here, the object is entirely useless, having no other function than to carry an engraving, and no one is expected to drink from it - unless perhaps it is intended for a chalice or loving cup, the exception to the rule. Call it simply a cylinder of glass on a rod, a tulip with a stalk, an inverted cone. As for quality, the quirks and slight discoloration so dear to the collector of antiques are mere imperfections to the point-engraver, who can indeed, and all too often must, involve and lose small obstacles in his design, opaque spots, fine sand, bubbles, wobbles or crazing, but whose ideal medium would be a perfectly colourless glass, perfectly free from all variations – an approach that will be shocking to the connoisseur for whom the design engraved comes second to shape and idiosyncracy.

Shape, all the same, can be a pleasure and is far from unimportant. Together with transparency it affords glass two unique advantages over all other pictorial mediums. But possibilities of shape are strictly limited. There are, first, the limitations of glass-blowing itself, where the hand must rely so much on skill and experience, so little on measurement; and within these there are the narrower limitations of the modern glass-blower, who possesses, for all we know, as much native talent as his predecessors in the great ages of craftsman-ship, but who is never now given full opportunity to exercise and enlarge it, so that anything out of the ordinary may be beyond him. But for this, one could devise more adventurous shapes – in terms of varied profile and proportion. For they would need always to be fairly simple. Any ornament in the glass itself, such as polished cutting or a twisted stem, not to mention the winged filigree of Venetian work, tends to detract from the less obtrusive picture, by competing with it in a multitude of reflections.

There are, finally, certain special requirements of the maker of pictures. In order that the scene may not be distorted, he needs for many subjects – and notably for architectural subjects – a bowl whose sides are vertical, or at least vertical for most of its height. Other subjects ask for other shapes. But broadly speaking those three types of bowl, the cylinder, the tulip and the reversed cone, will supply, in the variations of form that are feasible, nearly all his needs.

[8]

Of the shapes blown to my design on these principles, six are represented in this book: they are listed below with the year of origin, and outline sketches of three of them are shown. The plate number refers to the earliest example of each illustrated in this book. All six were first made for me by Whitefriars Glass Ltd. The exact height may vary from goblet to goblet.

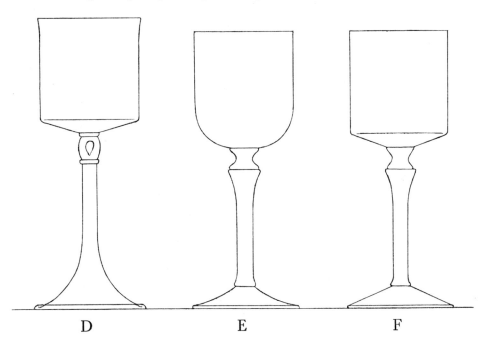

D   E   F

A *Cylinder*. On a cone-shaped stem. 9 inches high and $3\frac{1}{2}$ inches in diameter. 1954. Plate 2.
B *Reversed Cone*. 9 inches high and 4 inches in top diameter. 1954. Plate 4.
C *Tulip*. On a baluster stem. 10 inches high and $5\frac{1}{4}$ inches in diameter. 1958. Only three were engraved. Plate 1.
D *Cylinder*. On a trumpet stem with folded foot. 10 inches high and $3\frac{5}{8}$ inches in diameter. 1960. Plate 8. See drawing above.
      Repeated by Leerdam, Holland in 1969. Also a few without folded foot, $9\frac{1}{2}$ inches high and $3\frac{1}{4}$ inches in diameter. Plate 59.
E *Tulip*. On a baluster stem. $9\frac{1}{2}$ inches high and $3\frac{1}{2}$ inches in diameter. 1968. Plate 42. See drawing above.
F *Cylinder*. On a baluster stem. $9\frac{1}{2}$ inches high and $3\frac{1}{2}$ inches in diameter. 1969. Plate 56. See drawing above.

These shapes provided most of the glasses reproduced. The remainder, including a decanter, were bought ready-made.

Ultimately shape is important because it is designed to carry pictures in the round, pictures curving in the vertical plane through 180° and more. And a curved picture is not to be thought of as a flat one bent: it is devised for those particular curves and would be different and probably inappropriate on others. The initial idea suggests the glass to be used, and is then worked out on that surface. Sometimes the glass suggests the initial idea, as when a bowl is imagined as a circular room. Less obviously than this, the picture can reflect, within itself, in some passage or some manner, the outline or character of bowl or stem, or both, so that a unity more felt than recognized may result from the close interaction between subject and medium.

But the prime consideration is transparency, the first characteristic of glass, which by making the whole circle of the bowl visible strongly suggests three-dimensional treatment. For a picture can be drawn, not only on what will be the far side, but inside the far side to the extent that the engraver can insert his hand, so that the two planes of drawing reinforce perspective, making far things far. Alternatively, the planes can be reversed so as to contradict perspective, making far things unnaturally near, as in Plate 23, 'Idea of a City'. On flat panels a scene can be divided more or less equally between front and back, as in Plates 38 and 65. If the picture is carried round the sides of the bowl it will begin to frame itself by appearing in front, and then all four surfaces can be engraved, as in Plate 41, 'From the Ruined Tower.' Or it can be reversible, like the subject in Plate 32, which is nightfall or daybreak according to position.

THE ENGRAVINGS in this my third book have been chosen from the work of twelve years, and begin where those in my second left off. None here is purely emblematic or inscriptional, though I have continued to do some work of this kind. None is purely topographical, though some, especially at the beginning, are derived from actual places. Mostly the subjects are imaginary, and record the steps of a struggle towards a certain kind of landscape. But here I have to touch on some notions that lie behind this attempt.

The world around us is full of meanings – the emotional meanings we impose on it, read into it, and half-believingly discover in it. In fact the external world, the particular settings in which a man lives out his life, whether by chance or choice, can be regarded as the given material into which he must infuse such meanings, into which he does infuse them constantly, whether he intends to or not. The most significant object is the human face, and the most influential face the first to be encountered, the face of the mother whose disapproval and approval, tenderness, irritation and laughter were recognizable almost before the features of her face itself. After those earliest readings in significance it is doubtful if we do not read expressions everywhere, and most clearly of all in comparatively simple objects where they are easily identified, a jug, an attaché case, a weather-vane, a croquet-hoop, a pylon. All round, things look at us. Even geometrical shapes display shadowy differences of mood and personality, one oblong from another, any oblong from a square, a circle from an ellipse, and that again from a true oval. If pressed we could probably find words for even these elusive differences, and they would probably agree to some extent. The less simple the context the greater the chance of disagreement, but what is curious is not that the meanings we infuse should be at variance, for that we should expect in so subjective a matter, but that they should have enough in common to be worth our exchanging, should be a topic of interest. Thus we may discuss whether a house is 'cheerful' or 'gloomy', or more rewardingly (since there the disagreement would be too great for much discussion), whether a house is really 'sinister' or merely 'melancholy'. At the opposite extreme are meanings so utterly at variance that it is odd a single set of externals can evoke them both, a single context contain them; and here the lapse of time can play a part. To visit a scene of recent horror seems morbid and repulsively callous. Yet in a place of torture and execution, long disused, we can be carefree. Myriads of sight-seeing visitors are, every year. The place for them has the meaning of a holiday, an outing; and this is so though another meaning is in mind – is the very reason for their going there. More often another meaning is not in mind, and by no means looked for; yet it may be quite recent. There must be few stretches of road where the scenery has not been imbued with the pity and anguish of an accident. Precisely the same surroundings can be saturated with terror for one, with joy for another, and with mere boredom or contentment for a third. It is the meanings that count. We look at what is, but respond to what it says: to what we make it say.

So much for the subjective. To ask if there is any objective meaning is to leave rational discussion behind for an appeal to the faith which is based on actual experience, and this faith is no more capable of disproof than of proof. Faith claims – it knows – that the good is beyond definition and only to be lived. It may be that existence is good in itself; that the universe has been or is being invented out of goodness, and for it; that 'Energy is Eternal Delight', as Blake said. It may be that the subjective and objective meanings ought to be in harmony, though capable of the infinitely varied combinations of happiness. If so, something seems wrong – wrong with our awareness surely – wrong with time, pain and death as we experience them. If not, there is really nothing: there are no meanings other than the ones we can invent and rub out in a change of mood: which means there are no meanings. But if so, happiness is the aim of awareness, and that object is hardly achieved. And to pursue happiness is futile, for it always proves to be a by-product. And too often happiness is something longed-for rather than acquired, lost almost as soon as it is found, remembered or foreseen rather than tasted. This is the predicament of every man, reflected in the meanings he reads into his surroundings, and those he expresses in the things he makes. If there is 'a' meaning, an objective, reliable, absolute, indestructible meaning indifferent to chance and mood, at best he only glimpses it. If there is none, there is nothing.

This is the predicament indeed of everyone who ponders, except those few who have entire certainty, one way or another. And these are not irrelevant thoughts, absurdly pretentious in such a context as this. As they underlie so much of modern living and doing, so they underlie these engravings. My aim, then, is to represent an actual scene, or more often an invented one, in such a way that it will seem to have significance, to make the looked-at have the look of being meant – whether the particular meaning is clear, as in obvious allegory, or doubtful. How is this to be done when the actual scenes of life, whatever they may ultimately mean, are capable of wearing contradictory meanings and being read several ways?

A hint of the answer can be taken from the kind of effect we often meet in our surroundings and dismiss at once as accidental. An object, say a wood on a hillside or a window in a wall, may appear too simple or too emphatic to be 'likely' or 'natural'. Ambiguities of shape occur. Outlines appear to cross. Things seem to wear expressions too obtrusively, or to point at one another, or consciously to 'rhyme', responding to each other in shape, where no relationship exists. Accidental it is, but it appears intended, breaking out from the profusion of nature and the randomness of things-as-they-are.

Certain elements in a scene can be simplified, and thereby given excessive emphasis. And this merely accords with what we do unconsciously, especially at times of heightened emotion: picking out sights, but also sounds, smells and textures, to carry the meaning of the hour or the moment – identifying emotion with the clatter of a falling bicycle, with a sky scribbled over by vapour-trails, with the smell of an alley – inscribing an argument in the grain of a tabletop with the invisible ink of concentration.

Rhyming and ambiguity can appear anywhere, but the best examples are to be seen in mountains and high hills, which anyway give, through distance and gratuitous enormity, like the sea, the strong impression of a meaning to be caught. There, outlines and masses answer one another as the same curve or angle is repeated or reversed, and sometimes the answering could almost make one laugh, as if some conscious playfulness were seen at work. If one moves through such scenery at a moderate pace, rhyming occurs in one place or another all the time; and it is remarkable how often the outlines appear to cross and the masses they define to be intelligible in two ways, either when a concave dips till it exactly kisses a convex rising from below, or when a far-off outline appears to be carried straight on by some fold or pattern in much nearer ground or by a momentary effect of light and shadow; for sun and cloud may be at work as well, reversing relative distances, bringing forward and setting back, making one of what was two, two of what was one, turning the whole panorama into transparencies laid one on another in succession. And then it seems that the forms and coloured patterns are unfolding in some obscure notation, and the meaning of the whole would be revealed as silent music – such a music as would be different in the lyrical outlines of chalk downs, the flame-shapes of the Appenines, or the long roofs of the Black Mountains in Wales.

In another effect, also not peculiar to high country, crossing outlines meet by coincidence at the very edge of some nearer object, as if it were held up for attention and pointed at. For things in the actual world point by accident, but in the depicted one on purpose. Any actual road invites us to travel: its pictured image can underline the invitation. Long shadows and long lights are index fingers. Leaning tree trunks reveal marked unanimity. Or a stalk of rye grass can describe that curve which is the very graph of transience, the curve of the fountain and the firework – the parabola and the parable of come-and-gone.

Perspective itself is evocative – the word being here applied to observable fact, the diminution of objects in proportion to their distance from the eye, and the convergence of parallel lines in recession. It is most evocative in the diminishing lines of long streets, straight railways and runways, telephone wires and high-tension cables, and therefore more so in the modern world than in any before it. Still, the Romans were familiar with the dwindling of military roads to the horizon and of aqueducts looping the Campagna, and knew its imperious pull. For perspective always pulls us from where we are to where we might be. Sometimes to no likely advantage: a grey street in a grey town directs us to nothing more obvious than additional greyness. But more often to apparent advantage. Something different, something not perfectly perceived, something unpossessed appeals from far off. 'There' is linked to 'here' so quickly and simply by sight, so laboriously, if at all, by travel. This is surely the main excitement of the view from high places, as of the far-off town at nightfall that breathes with street-lamps and unshareable activity. The other hills, the ones we do not walk on, are unattainable. Ours might be viewed as temptingly from them, but it makes no difference. We want wings: also to stoop on our way and caress the quilted fields and almost stationary traffic. Aeroplanes have the beauty of cloudscape, but no sense of a linked 'here' and 'there', because passengers exist in another world from what they look at. Trains with their sideways-looking have only the 'there-there-there' of the unexpected, sensuously thrilling at speed. When cars are given up, as they ought to be, it may be

[13]

forgotten that sometimes, in ideal conditions of little or no traffic, they came near to supplying instant possession without stress, as they liquefied an entire prospect and made attainable horizons.

Another possibility is the use throughout a picture of a dominant form, which may be derived from the shapes of the glass itself, as I have said, or else from some feature in the scene depicted, or again from some interchange of light and shadow; for light and the wind create meaning in any landscape they scan, as they ponder each feature in turn, or, with startling speed, one end and then the other of a street.

But these, after all, are only aids and devices. To exploit the accidents of observation, to subject representation to an abstract idea, is only useful in the interests of something else. The pictures here are representational but are not concerned with scenery for its picturesque qualities (as that word is now generally understood): this is true of the later ones, at least. The kind of meanings I have tried for are these. – That life is a matter of moments, once-only and unrepeatable; that awareness of the moment is precious, and heightened awareness has the quality of a dream, simplifying and isolating from alternative readings. That the meaning can be good, is good, but is only to be glimpsed and otherwise groped for and remembered. That the meaning, as things are, can be also evil. That the important questions are those asked by children of themselves and abandoned by adults because they grow indifferent to there being no answers. That the light needs the dark to be intelligible. That ambiguity prevails.

Glass is an ideal medium for expressing the ambiguous, having ambiguity in its very nature. In theory it should be still in a liquid state, we are told, or at least viscous: in practice it feels hard enough. It can last unaltered for a thousand years, or be destroyed at a touch. It is there, and not there. That this is no flight of fancy will be confirmed by any connoisseur who has banged an antique rummer into the front of a cabinet supposedly open, or by anyone who is thankful to be only bruised after walking through a plate-glass door. Full of illusion itself, glass calls for an illusionistic art, and would do so even if this could be banned in all visual arts by the fiat of fashion. When engraved, it can be made to distinguish sharply between light and darkness, but when held to the light all distinctions disappear: there is no darkness. Gradually through years one begins to learn what to say in glass, by discovering, for oneself and within one's own limited capacity, what glass is capable of saying.

Notes on the Plates

FRONTISPIECE. CORINTHIAN WOOD. The trees of the wood rise into columns and entablatures. In the distance the temple columns rise to form a roof of trees. A back-engraving of 1971. 10 inches high and 3⅝ inches in diameter. *See also plate 67.*

PLATE 1. THE MAUSOLEUM. Derived from Hawksmoor's masterpiece at Castle Howard (see note to Plate 2), but of simpler outline at the base. Silhouetted by lightning and rain, with tossing trees beyond, the building itself is unengraved: the scene can be viewed from either side, but is intended to be treated as a back-engraving. The goblet, to the artist's design, is 10 inches high and 5¼ inches in diameter. 1960. *The Victoria and Albert Museum, London*

PLATE 2. THE TEMPLE RESTORED. A moonlight view of Vanbrugh's Temple at Castle Howard, engraved as a family present to Mr George Howard, to mark the restoration of the building. Hawksmoor's Mausoleum appears in the distance. A front-engraving of 1959. The goblet, blown to the artist's design, is 9 inches high and 3¼ inches in diameter. *George Howard Esq.*

PLATE 3. HEVER CASTLE. A moonlit view for the late Lord Astor of Hever, front-engraved in 1960 as a pair to a glass of 1957, reproduced in *Engraved Glass 1952–1958.* 9 inches high and 3¾ inches in diameter.

PLATE 4. POPE JOHN XXIII. The papal crown and keys appear on the foot of the glass. A front-engraving of 1961, 9 inches high, and 4 inches in top diameter. *Jeffrey Rose Esq.*

PLATE 5. CHRISTMAS IN ENGLAND. The old English version of the Christmas Tree. The globe is constructed of fine wire circles covered with box, containing sixteen red candles evenly spaced, and in the centre seven red apples hanging level on ribbons. The mistletoe hangs below. Back-engraved on a goblet of the artist's design in 1961. 9 inches high, and 4 inches in top diameter. *Mrs D. Binns*

PLATE 6. STATION DAYBREAK. A railway station in remote country. The ends of two platforms. No train as yet signalled. Old moon and morning star. The time is early dawn – or almost sunrise – according to the amount of light thrown on the glass. A back-engraving of 1960. 8¾ inches high and 3½ inches in diameter. *L. de Rothschild Esq.*

[15]

PLATE 7a (top). CANTERBURY CATHEDRAL FROM NEAR TONFORD. A glass slab for the late Christopher Hassall, engraved in 1961 with the view from near his garden at Tonford Manor. The edge of the slab carries the inscription. About 4 inches by 2¾ inches.   *Miss Joan Hassall*

PLATE 7b (foot). THE SACRED GROVE. Supernatural light in a circle of trees. A spring issuing below. A back-engraving of 1962. 10¼ inches high and 3½ inches in diameter.

PLATE 8. THE BENEDICTION. Halsdon Mill in Devon from the field called Venstave: shown in the loop of an ankh, the symbol of blessing and happiness. A back-engraving of 1963. 10½ inches high and 3½ inches in diameter.   *The Corning Museum of Glass, New York, USA*

PLATE 9. THE RADCLIFFE GATEWAY, UNIVERSITY COLLEGE, OXFORD. A decanter engraved as a present from undergraduates to Mrs Goodhart, the wife of the Master, on his retirement in 1963.
          Mrs Goodhart

PLATE 10. MOUNT OMEGA. So called, because the form of the final Greek letter appears on its marble or snowy flank (not clearly seen in the photograph). The mountain is also emblematically the end, and therefore viewed across the waters of death. Yet the light issues from it, not from the blackened sun, and allusion is made to Teilhard de Chardin's 'Omega-point', as the end and focus of all consciousness; beyond time: 'Not only does it crown but it closes.' This is a back-engraving, but the mountain itself is on the inside of the back. Thus, being a fraction of an inch in front of the sky, it seems to float at an uncertain distance. 1963. 10 inches high and 3⅝ inches in diameter.
          Lady Labouchere

PLATE 11. RICH DEATH. A spectral ash tree has the stars of the night sky for blossom, while its roots enfold a buried coffin. A symbol of the unity of the universe, with a suggestion of personal immortality. A front-engraving of 1962. 9 inches high and 4 inches in top diameter.   *Sir Hugh Dawson, Bart.*

PLATE 12. LONGFORD CASTLE IN AN IMAGINARY SETTING. The inscription reads: 'Presented to the Earl of Radnor on his retirement as Chairman, 1952–1963, by the Forestry Commission' – some parts of this being written down the trees at each side. These trees, broad-leaved to the left, conifers to the right, curve round to the front of the glass, though the picture is otherwise on the back. The castle itself is on the inside of the back, as if in mid-air. 10 inches high and 3⅝ inches in diameter.   *The Dowager Countess of Radnor*

PLATE 13. THE TOUCH OF DAY. The moment of sunrise for the house in the combe – Halsdon Mill, North Devon. A back-engraving of 1963, 10 inches high and 3½ inches in diameter. Another version of this glass, without the hands of sunlight and called 'The Moment of Waking', was reproduced in the artist's account of his first marriage, *The Initials in the Heart*, 1964.

Timothy Clarke Esq.

PLATES 14 AND 15. THE SLANTED LIGHT. Early morning, as yet empty of man – an imaginary landscape of 1963, back-engraved on a glass 10 inches high and 3⅝ inches in diameter. A near-replica, of the same year, was called 'The Slanting Light'.

Mrs Felix Fenton

PLATES 16 AND 17. AGAINST THE DAY. A yew tree stands black against the sunlight, its points reflecting the pinnacles of a church tower that rises into light from the deep valley to one side. Another answers in the distance. There is a double meaning in the title, for the yew which blocks the sunlight with its sombre shape is also the evergreen symbol of resurrection. The hills, curving down each side, hold the yew and the distant tower exactly between two points. Front-engraved in 1964 on a glass 10 inches high.

The Glenbow Museum, Calgary, Alberta

PLATE 18. DRIVING WESTWARDS. A cathedral spire against the sunset, at the hour when the neon signs along the road look pale as jewels, an effect they lose after nightfall. The street-lamps diminish to suggest movement into the distance. The cone-shaped glass, of the artist's designing, reflects the spire. A back-engraving of 1964. 9 inches high and 4 inches in top diameter.

The Earl of Dalhousie

PLATE 19. BLAGDON, NORTHUMBERLAND. The urn is one that stands near the house; but its pedestal is here made to carry the inscription 'M.W.R. 1902–1964', for this glass was given to the late Lady Ridley in memory of her husband, Lord Ridley, by the North-Eastern Housing Association, to record his directorship. A back-engraving, 10 inches high and 3⅝ inches in diameter.

PLATES 20 AND 21. AND SUMMER AND WINTER. The title is continuous, running all round the foot of the goblet, to suggest the unending seasons. A thatched cottage by a stream appears twice over, as if mirrored: in Spring sunrise, and under snow. Between the two is a grove of trees. To the left the trunks are dark, being silhouetted against brightness. But solid and space change places somewhere in the middle, and to the right the light strips become the trees themselves, covered with snow. This ambiguity was suggested by the work of the Dutch artist, M. C. Escher: in particular by a drawing of

[17]

birds called 'Day and Night'. A front-engraving of 1965. 10 inches high and 3⅝ inches in diameter.   *E. Korner Esq.*

PLATE 22. GLENALMOND. Given to Princess Chichibu at the commissioning of the SS Glenalmond (see description of Plate 26). The view is of the lower Glen, looking north. A back-engraving of 1966, 10 inches high and 3⅝ inches in diameter.

PLATE 23. IDEA OF A CITY. An allegory. Two lovers regard their future in a visionary landscape, whose lines issue from their eyes and mouths, to show they are creating it together, by seeing and saying it to one another. The picture is a back-engraving, but the city to which the road leads down and up is engraved on the inside of the back, and thus floats at an uncertain distance. All the light in the picture comes from the city. Its architecture is of no particular date. The lines of trees issuing from the lovers' eyes extend to the mountains behind; and, in reverse, the mountains flow out of their foreheads. 1966. 10 inches high and 3⅝ inches in diameter.   *Raymond Lister Esq.*

PLATES 24 AND 25. FROM THE DEAD TO THE QUICK. The trees come round both sides of the bowl so that we seem to be looking into and then out of a circular grove. The nearer side is Death, the farther side Life. On the nearer they are rotted and fungus-grown, and between them stretches a line of rubbish, as if from a refuse-dump. On the farther side they are in Spring leaf. But the trees are like those on the glass called 'And Summer And Winter' (see description of Plates 20 and 21), with solid and space gradually changing places.

On the far side of the bowl a sunrise scene contains the same looped symbol of felicity, the ankh, seven times over. But whereas in Egyptian wall-reliefs the ankh is extended on the end of a visible sunray, here each one, though pointing to the sun, is formed by certain features in the landscape, as if accidentally – by crossed twigs on the trees, crossed grasses, the shape of a hill, a hedge or a cliff, or a domed building, etc. The meaning is that felicity is in the landscape itself – or rather in the eye that would discover it there. 1968. 10 inches high and 3⅝ inches in diameter.   *Spencer Le Marchant Esq.*

PLATE 26. MAGDALEN COLLEGE, OXFORD. Sunrise, with morning traffic flowing in across the bridge, and a kingfisher flying up-stream. The top of the tower is lit on the shadow-side also, as if its masonry had absorbed the early light. The glass was given to Princess Chichibu in 1966 when she launched the 'Glenalmond', built in Nagasaki for the Blue Funnel Line. Prince Chichibu had been an undergraduate at the College. A front-engraving, 10 inches high and 3⅝ inches in diameter.

PLATE 27. FROCWARD CARSELBAR. The name is an anagram of Crawford (and) Balcarres. A glass given to Lord Crawford by the National Trust on his retirement as Chairman in 1966. It was pretended that the goblet merely recorded the gift to him, outright, of an actual estate in the care of the Trust – the imaginary one depicted here. The artist therefore wrote a fictitious architectural history of Frocward, which appeared with photographs in *The Connoisseur* of June 1967.

Briefly, this essay presented Frocward as a medieval castle with four round towers, partly rebuilt in Jacobean times, and given a new entrance front by Vanbrugh in 1724. At Frocward, his last work, the Vanbrugh style is taken a stage further than elsewhere, notably in the use of machicolations with a classical order. Vanbrugh also designed the Belvedere on the hill, a breakthrough into the frankly asymmetrical. In the foreground is the Little Palladian Bridge of 1738, one pavilion of Lord Herbert's famous bridge at Wilton.

The entrance piers are on the front of the bowl, leading by way of a short avenue to the landscape on the back; for this is in the main a back-engraving. A National Trust sign, recording the gift, is to the right. More information on the architecture of Frocward was given in the article already mentioned. 10 inches high and 3⅝ inches in top diameter.

The Earl of Crawford and Balcarres

PLATES 28 AND 29. THROUGH THE GATE OF A DREAM. Derived from a dream of the artist's, in which someone at twilight looked out of an upper window at a fire burning in a courtyard, and a black hawk hovering. The setting is derived from Dowland in North Devon, with Dartmoor behind the tower. It is viewed through an open gate in a bank, hairy with grasses each side, and also transparent, as though the dream were the gateway to some truth. The fire is engraved on the inside of the back, the remainder on the outside. 1966. 10 inches high and 3⅝ inches in diameter. *K. A. Alexander Esq.*

PLATES 30 AND 31. THE BANK OF ENGLAND. Two glasses given to Lord Cromer, on his retirement from the Governorship, by the London Discount Market Association, in 1967. 10 inches high and 3⅝ inches in diameter.

Plate 30 shows the interior of the Bank as it was, the old Colonial Office designed by Sir John Soane. Plate 31 shows the exterior of the Bank as it is – but placed on a cliff-edge withstanding the storm: a reference to the nation's financial crisis of the previous year, and an act of rescue performed by the Bank. The word 'Allegory' is written across itself in reverse, to show that this is a two-way glass that can be viewed as front- or back-engraved.

PLATE 32. DORSET NIGHTFALL – WESSEX DAYBREAK. The road and its cat's-eyes are lit by a car's headlamps. In the sky is a bull's-horn moon. Knobbed hills and the sea suggest the skyline of Dorset, seen against sunrise – or, alternatively, against sunset – for this is a two-way picture. When the engraving is in front the moon is new and the hour is nightfall (as the inscription says, to be read from that side). When the bowl is reversed it is the old moon, and the time daybreak (and then the other inscription applies). 1968. A Czechoslovakian glass, $4\frac{7}{8}$ inches high.   *J. G. Cluff Esq.*

PLATES 33, 34 AND 35. A SEASONS CENTREPIECE. A glass and silver-gilt device designed by the artist for the Goldsmiths' Company, and built by Leslie Durbin in 1968. At the top a small oval of glass, half-sun, half-sunflower, stands for the giving and receiving of light. The four wings below can be revolved by hand, or, when the centrepiece is placed on its separate plinth of gilt-bronze, by a low-gear electric motor hidden in this base.

The four panels, cut from a large sphere of glass, are slightly curved in section, and are face-forwards when seen to the left of the pillar. Each picture is then mainly on the back of the panel, but also partly in front, for the illusion of depth that results. Each illustrates a season, also a time of day, as follows:

Plate 34 (top). Spring afternoon. Sunlight and shadow of April over blossoming trees, and a hill derived from Skirrid Fawr in South Wales. Here only the rainbow and the veil of rain are engraved on the front. 'Spring' is written in the corn-shoots.

Plate 34 (foot). Summer sunrise, with a clear sky over dark trees and ripening wheat. The nearest ears, like the insects and the spider's web, are on the front.

Plate 35 (top). Autumn and late morning. A walk on the edge of a town, with a boy seen far off, playing by himself. Some of the sunshafts and falling leaves are on the front. A street-sign on the wall of the dark entry says 'Autumn Passage'.

Plate 35 (foot). Winter and late evening, with a distant town under snow, and one window lit in a hill-farm. Here the falling snow is on both sides of the glass. The name 'Winter' appears in bird-prints.

A fuller description was published in *Country Life* for June 20, 1968. $17\frac{1}{2}$ inches high: 14 inches wide. Each panel $4\frac{1}{4}$ inches by $6\frac{1}{4}$ inches.

PLATES 36 AND 37. EXACT TIME: APPOINTED PLACE. A car waits at twilight beside a country road, with lights extinguished, as if for a rendezvous. The place is where the line of the road runs up into the spire, and where the sides of the barn-gable exactly meet and are extended by two crossing hills. The time is when the new moon, seen from this spot, exactly balances on top of the spire. These are like precise co-ordinates: there can be no other place and moment in the world like this. Thus the theme is the uniqueness, the once-onliness of experience. The picture has other correspondences: the radiator of the old Lanchester and the roof of the barn; the headlamp immediately below the moon, etc. It is made of sharp angles with softer, rounded forms. 1968. 10 inches high and $3\frac{5}{8}$ inches in diameter.

Mrs E. Hill

PLATES 38 AND 39. THE FESTIVAL. For the golden wedding in 1968 of Sir Hugh and Lady Dawson. An oval of glass, $5\frac{3}{4}$ inches by $4\frac{3}{8}$ inches, held in a gilt-bronze frame which combines the shape of a heart with that of an ankh. The floodlit trees, the canal and the nearer fountains are engraved in front; the three tall jets, the mountains and the sky on the back. Throughout this design and its frame the basic form is the parabola, primarily that of the fountains, but seen also in the mountain-shapes, the lights of hill-villages, and the wrought-iron parapet with its cipher of 'H' and 'V.D'. The trident, whose three points answer the big fountains, denotes a naval career. The glass is 14 inches high and $5\frac{1}{2}$ inches wide. The frame was built by Leslie Durbin.

PLATE 40. REREDOS IN SHERBORNE ABBEY, DORSET. Three glass panels, framed in bronze doors and about 4 feet high by 10 feet wide, engraved as a reredos for the Lady Chapel. The engraving, lit by concealed tube-lighting above and below, shows white against a background of jet-black velvet, some eight inches behind.

The theme is glory and plenty. Emblems of the Virgin Mary are seen. In the centre is her winged heart pierced with a sword. Its point is centred on a new moon, a pagan symbol of fruitfulness, taken over in her name. So is the point of the big M. whose arms, curving round, evolve into cornucopias overflowing with wheat and grapes, symbols of food and drink, and of the Sacrament. The hilt of the sword rises to her jewelled crown, ringed in light and topped with lilies and roses – one rose aflame. The forms of this crown reflect the same heart-shape, as do also the inner and outer circlets of stars.

The execution was as follows. Under the direction of the artist the main features were first engraved in light sandblast on quarter-inch plate glass by the craftsmen of T. & W. Ide Ltd. The engraver then worked over the whole design, adding also the wings, the vine, the nimbus of the crown, the veins or fronds on the heart. These last were derived from the lines of stress in certain substances, as revealed by X-ray photography. The central star (for Stella Maris) and the main jewels of the crown, being deep-cut and polished, look black or bright-faceted according to the angle of vision.

Above the reredos a beam, designed by the engraver, repeats the rhythms in the glass below, with raised machicolations answered by a sequence of 'M's and crowns, linked together, alternate. These were painted in black by William Anstice Brown.

The reredos was completed in 1969 for the farewell service of the Vicar, Canon Wingfield Digby, whose idea it had been. A fuller description appeared in *Country Life* for May 8, 1969.

PLATE 41. FROM THE RUINED TOWER. The bowl itself constitutes the tower as we look across it – in through one gap and out of the other. This is a development in form of Plates 24 and 25, 'From the Dead to the Quick', where also the distant scenery is framed twice over. But here the broken circle of trees is replaced by masonry, and all four surfaces of the glass are engraved: the nearer edges of stonework are on the outside and inside of the front; the farther edges on the inside of the back; while the landscape beyond is on the outside. This was to give remoteness to the landscape, and especially to the distant town, which hangs in darkness as if supported by the hovering gulls, and towards which three poplars point from below. 1968. 10 inches high and $3\frac{5}{8}$ inches in diameter.   *Lady Elizabeth Dewar*

PLATE 42. VALSE TRISTE. Buildings have human expressions, sometimes even faces. Also a photograph of a building at the moment of demolition can bring home what the onlooker's eye would hardly register: that the upper part of it stays stolidly intact, sees nothing amiss on the brink of complete dissolution. Even as it falls it could be rescued by a miracle. This gives the touch of horror to such photographs – by analogy with the moment before some human disaster. A front- or back-engraving of 1969. $9\frac{1}{2}$ inches high and $3\frac{1}{2}$ inches in diameter.   *Mark Birley Esq.*

PLATE 43. CHI-RHO AT TWILIGHT. The passage of the new moon behind three grass-blades forms for a moment the symbol that is made from the first two letters, in Greek, of the name Christos. A signpost points to the lights of a town or village (round the right-hand side of the bowl). A front-engraving of 1968. $7\frac{1}{2}$ inches high.   *Mrs Birch*

PLATES 44 AND 45. THE ENCOUNTER. A man and a woman approach one another down a gallery with no visible end, which at the same time appears to be a bridge. The coved ceiling is painted with flowers, fireworks, birds, stars, a book, masks, fountains, etc. The floor has a pattern of linked ankhs for good fortune; and of lyres where the two will meet. Urns of flowers mark the seasons, alternating with seats. Birds mate outside and butterflies inside. Sunlight pours through the windows. But the wall opposite is blank, with a plain door.

The theme is related to that of 'Exact Time: Appointed Place' (Plates 36 and 37), but here the meeting is explicit. The idea was partly derived from the bridge-gallery at Chenonceaux. A back-engraving of 1969. 10 inches high and 3⅝ inches in diameter. *Oliver Dawnay Esq.*

PLATE 46. HIGH NOON. Suddenly entered, a wood in bright sunlight seems black and white. Ferns mimic the twist of the road, and telegraph wires sketch the way downhill. 1968. 9½ inches high and 3½ inches in diameter.

PLATE 47. MAN-SPATE. Release or escape. The traffic sweeps one way down an artery whose curve is defined by street lamps and the silhouettes of buildings, under a sky that could be bright with sunset, or with actual flames. A back-engraving of 1969. 9½ inches high and 3½ inches in diameter.

M. Wayne Field Esq.

PLATES 48 AND 49. MOUNT OF OLIVES. A figure stands or kneels among tree-trunks that assume demonic forms of mockery. The night-sky is full of signs and wonders. The world curves round below, turning into waves that make the mount seem an island in a sea. A tilted ring of radiance encircles the whole scene and the glass itself. There is an allusion here to Henry Vaughan's couplet:

I saw Eternity the other night
Like a great Ring of pure and endless light

A back-engraving of 1969. 9½ inches high and 3½ inches in diameter. *Mrs Hall*

PLATE 50. THE SIX OF SUMMER. A straight road through a tunnel of trees, with six intervals of sunlight. They spiral forward, growing farther apart, to a final dark hole like the shutter of a camera, suggesting perhaps observation the other way on. The name suggests a playing card – something dealt by chance, and gratuitous. A back-engraving of 1969. 10 inches high and 3⅝ inches in diameter.

PLATE 51. A SENSE OF SUMMER. The walls are transparent, a stream falls into and across the room, yew boughs lean towards the bed, a white bird flies out into their shadows. The room has been dissolved for the couple inside it by awareness of Summer going on outside. One of them works at a table. Against the knees of the other a book is propped open at the title-page: it gives the title of the glass. But the frontispiece held open by a hand shows exactly the same scene in miniature. And the same hand appears, big, to the left of the room itself, as if that in turn were a frontispiece. So a series is implied, in both directions. At every stage upwards the room may be a picture in a larger book, at every stage downwards the page portrays a smaller room. The meaning is the serial nature of awareness. The receptive mind is aware, and aware of being aware . . . Also, to the figure on the bed these moments are like something to read, and like something being read elsewhere. A back-engraving of 1969. 10 inches high and 3⅝ inches in diameter.

PLATE 52. THE AVENUE WATCHED. It has been cut short by the encroaching town. One house looks up the avenue as if awaiting whatever may emerge. The town has eaten back into the trees, but the trees may have the last word. A back-engraving of 1969. 9½ inches high and 3½ inches in diameter.

Mr and Mrs Ralph Walker

PLATE 53. THE WISHED-FOR. One shaft of light towards evening holds for a moment the Grail, here given a wider significance than that of sacred legend, and meant as a symbol of all that is seriously or passionately desired. Forms cross and merge in a landscape that is not wholly real. The theme was suggested by an effect of light across the Kenmare River, seen from near the top of the Healey Pass in Kerry. A back-engraving of 1969. 9½ inches high and 3⅝ inches in diameter.

Laurence Irving Esq.

PLATE 54. FROM CASTLE TO AIRPORT. Given to H.M. The Queen by the British Airports Authority in 1970: a glass dish, framed upright in an oval of gilt-bronze on a pillar, rather similar in shape to that in Plate 39, and also built by Leslie Durbin, the glass being of the same size, 5¾ inches by 4⅜ inches. On the back is engraved an aerial view of Windsor Castle, the M4 to the left, the Thames, and the distant airport among clouds. The nearer clouds are on the front.

Her Majesty The Queen

PLATE 55. WELSH FARM. Lamplit window – gable end – and moon over a round mountain. Suggested by a farm at Pontesgob, below the Sugar Loaf in South Wales. Back-engraved in 1970. 9½ inches high and 3¼ inches in diameter.

PLATES 56 AND 57. WET LANE TOWARDS EVENING. A Devon landscape, though imaginary, held in balance by three points of light, the valley, the sea, and the top of the streaming lane as it rises towards sunshine. A back-engraving of 1969. 9½ inches high and 3½ inches in diameter. *Mrs Bond*

PLATE 58. THE WHITE WATER. A waterfall below a mountain, marble-white in the sun, the landscape chequered by light and shadow. A back-engraving of 1970. 10 inches high and 3⅝ inches in diameter.

PLATE 59. THE GAY MAUSOLEUM. It stands, beflagged, on a hill-top, with the landscape seeming to extend from it: between bare rocks and trees, the sterile and the fertile, and answered by the far country beyond them. Back-engraved in 1970. 9½ inches high and 3¼ inches in diameter.

PLATES 60 AND 61. THE TEMPLE OF NIGHT AND DAY. It stands on a hill-top above Megalopolis, stretching to the horizon, the limitless city of the future. But the steps have crumbled and the way up is forgotten. Its columns, interchanging solid and space like the trees in Plate 25, cannot be counted. It guards within it, or below it, suspended from the portico, another notion of night and day, Edenic or Arcadian. A back-engraving of 1970. 10 inches high and 3⅝ inches in diameter.

PLATES 62 AND 63. THE EVENING PLANE. The view is from the cove at Rovinia, on the west coast of Corfu, with a cave to the left, and the vapour-trail of the Athens plane rising up over Paleokastritsa. A back-engraving of 1970. 10 inches high and 3⅝ inches in diameter. *Robert Wessel Esq.*

PLATE 64. A VANBRUGH WEMYSS. A window-pane for Wemyss Castle on the Firth of Forth, given by Andrew and David Wemyss to their parents, on their Golden Wedding in 1970. It pretends to show Vanbrugh's revision of the South and West fronts – with the sea and sky shining through them, since the project came to nothing. Vanbrugh's complete reconstruction of the castle, from drawings supposedly discovered, was published as a hoax in an article by the engraver, appearing in *Country Life* for June 10, 1971. The pane, drill-engraved, is 12 inches high and 9½ inches wide. The photograph was taken before insertion. *Michael Wemyss Esq.*

PLATE 65. EASTON NESTON. The view is of Hawksmoor's garden facade as seen from the dark avenue across the pool. House and sky are on the back of the glass, lawn and trees on the front, the parterre being simplified, and a dreamlike effect intended. Drill-engraved on plate glass about 12½ inches high and 10 inches wide, for a window on the side depicted, and given by Lady Hesketh to her eldest son. 1971. The photograph was taken before the pane was put in.

PLATE 66. A KIND OF ALTARPIECE. In the round room the table is laid in front of an open window, with a landscape beyond. The nearer opening, of white masonry, is on the front of the glass, the remainder on the back. 1971. 10 inches high and 3⅝ inches in diameter.

PLATE 67. CORINTHIAN WOOD. *See note on the frontispiece.*

PLATE 68. A WINDOW TO EDWARD AND HELEN THOMAS. A memorial to the poet and his wife in the parish church of Eastbury, near

Lambourn in Berkshire. In this village Helen Thomas spent the last twelve years of a fifty-years' widowhood that dated from the battle of Arras in 1917. She is buried at the top of the churchyard, where a row of beeches was planted soon afterwards.

Between the trees, one in bud, one bare, formal hands of sunlight confer a blessing on their names. Their initials and dates are on the bark of the Spring tree: on the Winter tree steel helmet and Sam Browne belt hang from a branch, to recall that this poet of the English countryside found his gift in war-time and wrote his poems chiefly as a soldier. In the distance can be seen the sarsen stone on the slope of a hill near Petersfield, with its memorial plaque to the poet – the spire of Steep church – and the cottage at Hodson Bottom in Wiltshire where the couple had been happy; and in the background the mountains of his Welsh origin. Lines from his poems, chosen by the engraver, are written across the landscape seemingly at random, so as to suggest the jottings of a poet in a notebook – or his thoughts in front of landscapes that inspired him:

> The glory invites me, yet it leaves me scorning
> All I can ever do, all I can be . . .
>
> Or must I be content with discontent
> As larks and swallows are perhaps with wings?
>
> I should use, as the trees and birds did
> A language not to be betrayed . . .
>
> Imperfect friends, we men
> And trees since time began; and nevertheless
> Between us still we breed a mystery . . .
>
> There I find my rest, and through the dusk air
> Flies what yet lives in me. Beauty is there . . .
>
> But what if I in them as they in me
> Nourished what has great value and no price?
>
> Perhaps
> I may love other hills yet more
> Than this . . .
>
> But the moment unveiled something unwilling to die
> And I had what most I desired . . .
>
> This is my grief. That land,
> My home, I have never seen;
> No traveller tells of it,
> However far he has been . . .

The titles of Helen Thomas's two books about their marriage, *As It Was* and *World Without End*, are engraved at each side.

[26]

The execution was like that of the Sherborne reredos (Plate 40): certain areas were given a very light sandblast tone, and on these, and other areas untouched, the artist engraved the picture with hand-tools, both pencil and drill. The main panels are 5 feet high, and each 19 inches wide, the total height being about 7 feet 6 inches. The ground-tone was provided by T. & W. Ide, Ltd.

After dark the window can be lit by flood-lighting outside. The effect then is that of this photograph, except that the upper part is as whitely engraved as the lower. The work was fully described in *Country Life* for October 7, 1971.

PLATE 69. WINDOW PANE AT STERNFIELD HOUSE, SUF-FOLK. For Lady Penn to give her husband, Sir Eric Penn, at their Silver Wedding in 1972. The house and background are on the back of the glass, the invented foreground in front. Under an Irish yew is the headstone, designed by the engraver and placed in the neighbouring churchyard, to Sir Eric's uncle, Sir Arthur Penn, who improved the house and garden. Drill engraved on plate glass about $21\frac{1}{2}$ inches high and 14 inches wide.

PLATE 70. SPRING MOON. Drill-engraved in 1971. 10 inches high and $3\frac{5}{8}$ inches in diameter.

PLATE 71. THE TUNNEL. At the frontier between town and countryside. A sunlit wood on the edge of industry. A railway below. $9\frac{1}{2}$ inches high and $3\frac{3}{8}$ inches in diameter. 1972.   *David Sheppard, Esq.*

PLATE 72. IN THE LIGHT OF MODERN PROGRESS. The title is ironical, but not entirely, for the temple is in fact only seen by the light from Megalopolis, rising ever higher around it, and shown here in reverse perspective – even as the Acropolis can only be approached from the view-point of modern Athens, spread like suds round the basin of the hills.

Allusion is made to the temple at Bassae in Arcadia, c. 430 BC, where the Corinthian order appears for the first time, a single votive column, central in the sanctuary; and where also the three classical orders, Doric, Ionic and Corinthian, uniquely appear together. However, it is not a picture of that temple; and in this and the following glass the intention is not to contrast ancient and modern as such. The classical orders are not proposed as an ideal form of architecture, but regarded as symbols of order itself, surrounded by chaos. A back-engraving of 1972. $9\frac{1}{2}$ inches high and $3\frac{1}{4}$ inches in diameter.

PLATE 73. THE LOST ORDER. The temple is submerged in the forest, but not as yet ruined – still intact. Perhaps the survivors of a sect help to keep it so. Sunlight penetrates the colonnade through leaves, and lights each morning the gold and ivory figure in the sanctuary, unseen.

Though not the source of this picture, the following sentence in W. C. Barrett's *What is Existentialism?* provides a comment: 'Man has not yet shown himself capable of controlling and shaping in some rational way the technological order, or disorder, that surrounds and strangles modern life like a rampant jungle of metallic liana plants.' Back-engraved in 1972. 10 inches high and $3\frac{1}{2}$ inches in diameter.

PLATE 74. THE GRASS CATHEDRAL. Grass into architecture: lit at the crossing. A back-engraving of 1972. 10 inches high and $3\frac{5}{8}$ inches in diameter.

PLATE 75. WAY OUT. A circular domed chamber shaped like a tholos tomb. Perhaps a prison; for the walls are covered with the initials and symbols of those who have spent time here, and the floor with their litter. There are two exits. All the light enters through the one marked 'Way'. It begins with easy steps, but would be hard to negotiate. Among those who have chosen this way of affirmation are certain poets, artists and composers. Dante Alighieri's stone has been left without addition, except (with becoming modesty) by 'T.S.E.' The other opening marked 'Out' provides an easy alternative into darkness, and has been vigorously embellished by many suicides, from Judas Iscariot, upside down, to the Nazi trio, and beyond. A back-engraving of 1971. $9\frac{1}{2}$ inches high and $3\frac{1}{2}$ inches in diameter.

PLATES 76 AND 77. ENTER. The round brick room has a door and a window. The door invites one to enter into a landscape of bright light, and a butterfly floats in the opening. But the landscape fits the doorway and seems hung from its corners. And the path turns immediately left above a sheer drop. Through the window to the left in another room a coffin is seen, shiny, with brass plate. A back-engraving of 1970. 10 inches high and $3\frac{5}{8}$ inches in diameter.

PLATES 78 AND 79. TRIPTYCH IN YEW WOOD. Three landscapes in the gaps between yew trees. To the left, childhood: a boy near a villa, watching a traction-engine. In the centre, youth: lovers on a bridge. To the right, age: an old man contemplating a terminal figure at the end of a tunnel. A back-engraving of 1971. 10 inches high and $3\frac{5}{8}$ inches in diameter.

PLATE 80. TERM. The scene at the end of the avenue in plate 79, where the yews open in a shape like the door to a tholos tomb. The sharp, terminal object rises from the hole it points at. Beyond, there is a landscape, which seems to be attached to the angles of the figure, and yet seems to be real. But it is upside down, as if obedient to another plane of reference. $9\frac{1}{2}$ inches high and $3\frac{3}{8}$ inches in diameter. 1972.

Bibliography

OF WORKS CONCERNED WITH THE ARTIST'S ENGRAVINGS

BOOKS BY LAURENCE WHISTLER

The Engraved Glass of Laurence Whistler	Cupid Press, 1952
Engraved Glass 1952-1958	Hart-Davis, 1959
The Initials in the Heart: The story of a marriage	Hart-Davis, 1964
A Point on Glass: Introduction to Catalogue	Agnew, 1969
Way: A glass and a sonnet by L.W.	Golden Head Press, 1969

REFERENCES IN BOOKS

The Collector's Dictionary of Glass by E. M. Elville	Country Life, 1961
Modern Glass by Ada Polak	Faber, 1962
A Manual on Etching and Engraving Glass by G. M. Heddle	Tiranti, 1961
Great Works of Craftsmanship by Raymond Lister	Bell, 1967

SELECTED ARTICLES

'Artist in Glass' by John Hadfield — *Saturday Book No. 10*, 1950

'A Masterpiece of British Craftsmanship' (The King's Casket) by Christopher Hussey — *Country Life*, 25 August 1950

'A Royal Triptych in Glass' by John Hadfield — *Country Life*, 23 January 1953

'The Queen's Homes in Glass' by John Hadfield — *Country Life*, 5 November 1953

'Laurence Whistler's Engraved Glass' by John Hadfield — *The Connoisseur*, October 1954

'Whistler Glass' — *Saturday Book No. 16*, 1956

'Engraved Goblets by Laurence Whistler' (for Trinity College, Oxford) by Sir Cecil Kisch — *The Connoisseur*, April 1957

'The Queen's Gift to the President' — *Country Life*, 11 April 1957

'Glass Engraving as a Fine Art' — *Illustrated London News*, 25 May 1957

'Church Windows by Laurence Whistler' (at Moreton, Dorset) by Patrick Macnaghten — *Country Life*, 15 January 1959

'With a Diamond on Glass' by the engraver — *Optima* (Anglo-American Corporation of South Africa), June 1960

'Landscapes on Glass' by John Hadfield — *Country Life*, 25 July 1963

'Recent Examples of the Work of Laurence Whistler' by Andrew Graham — *The Connoisseur*, June 1965

'The National Trust Bestows an Estate' — *The Connoisseur*, June 1967

'Laurence Whistler's Four Seasons' by M.B.   *Country Life*, 20 June 1968
'Timeless Emblems and Modern Skills' by Patrick Macnaghten
                                                   Country Life, 1969
'Pictures on Glass by Laurence Whistler'   *Saturday Book No. 30*, 1970
'A Vanbrugh Wemyss' by the engraver   *Country Life*, 10 June 1971
'Tribute to a Poet' by Noel Carrington   *Country Life*, 7 October 1971

Glasses in Public Galleries

The Victoria and Albert Museum, London: *The Mausoleum*
The Brighton Art Gallery: *The Fairy Palace*
The Royal Scottish Museum, Edinburgh: *Dawn of Emblems*
The Bristol City Art Gallery: *The Tor*
The Glenbow Museum, Calgary, Alberta: *Against the Day*
The Corning Museum of Glass, New York: *The Baroque of Collapse*, and
    The Benediction
The Fitzwilliam Museum, Cambridge: *To be chosen*

Engraved Window-glass and Glass Panels

In Churches
Moreton, Dorset. Five windows in the apse. 1958
Checkendon, Oxfordshire. Memorial window to Eric Kennington. 1962
Thannington, Kent. Memorial diamond pane to Christopher Hassall. 1963
RAF Hospital Chapel, Wegberg, Germany. Door panel. 1964 (Removed to
    England)
Ilton, Somerset. Memorial window to Henry Cecil Graham. 1967
Sherborne Abbey, Dorset. Reredos in the Lady Chapel. 1968
Uplyme, Devon. Two memorial panels in a wall-cabinet. 1970
Eastbury, Berkshire. Memorial window to Edward and Helen Thomas. 1971
The Guards' Chapel, London. The Welsh Guards' window. 1971

In Private Houses and Other Buildings
(Window-panes unless otherwise described)
Blagdon, Northumberland. For Lady Ridley. 1935
Campion Hall, Oxford. 1936
The Drum, Cockington, Devon. 1936
Mells, Somerset. For Lady Horner. 1936
27 Hasker Street, London, SW3. For Mr Christopher Hassall. 1936

Clovelly Court, Devon. For Mrs Asquith. 1936

The King's School, Canterbury. For Captain Duncan Stirling. 1938

Venton, Dolton, N. Devon. For Miss Jill Furse. 1939

Combe, Oxford. For Mr Ian Robertson. 1939

Fulvens Farm, Abinger Hammer, Surrey. For Mrs Webbe. 1939

8 Southwood Lane, Highgate. For Mr Christopher Hassall. 1939

Skipworth Hall, Yorkshire. For Mr Forbes Adam. 1939

Halsdon Mill, Dolton, N. Devon. 1940

General's Farm, Chartley, Staffordshire. For Mr and Mrs Christopher Congreve. 1943

Halsdon Mill, Dolton, N. Devon. Three panes with verses. 1944

South End House, Montpelier Row, Twickenham. For Mr Walter de la Mare. 1949

Mottisfont Abbey, Hampshire. For Mrs Russell. Three fingerplates and two bell-pushes. 1953

Hanover Bank, Mount Street, London. Screen of three panels. 1957 (Taken to New York)

New Zealand Shipping Co., Leadenhall Street, London. Glass door and panel. 1958

Armourers' Hall, London. Two door panels and two finger-plates. 1959

Hinton Ampner Place, Hampshire. For Captain Duncan Stirling. 1960

Munden, Watford. For Lord Knutsford. 1962

Ringdale Manor, Faringdon, Berkshire. For Sir James Walker. 1964

Drapers' Hall, London. 1964

Halsdon, Dolton, N. Devon. For Sir Ralph Furse. 1964

Balliol College, Oxford. 1965

Wemyss Castle, Fife. For Mr Michael Wemyss. 1970

Dyers' Hall, London. Two panels. 1971

Easton Neston, Northants. For Lady Hesketh. 1971

Sternfield House, Saxmundham, Suffolk. For Sir Eric and Lady Penn. 1972

Main Exhibitions

The Festival Hall, London. 1962. Seven exhibits. (With seven by Simon Whistler, and others)

Agnew's, London. May–June 1969. 'A Point on Glass'. Thirty exhibits. (With three by Simon Whistler)

The Haye, Lyme Regis. 25–26 June 1970. Fourteen exhibits. (With drawings and paintings by Rex Whistler)

Kettle's Yard, Cambridge. 9–27 November 1971. Nineteen exhibits. (With six by Simon Whistler)

The Plates

Except where a goblet, decanter, window-
pane or panel is illustrated in its entirety
the engravings are reproduced in exactly
the same size as the originals.

1 (opposite). THE MAUSOLEUM. 1960

2. THE TEMPLE RESTORED. Celebrating the renovation of Vanbrugh's Temple at Castle Howard. 19

3. HEVER CASTLE BY MOONLIGHT. 1960

4. POPE JOHN XXIII. 1961

5. CHRISTMAS IN ENGLAND: the Kissing Bough. 1961

6. STATION DAYBREAK. 1960

7a (opposite, above). CANTERBURY CATHEDRAL FROM NEAR TONFORD. 1961

7b (opposite, below). THE SACRED GROVE. 1962

8. THE BENEDICTION: Halsdon Mill, Devon, in the loop of an ankh. 1963

9. THE RADCLIFFE GATEWAY, UNIVERSITY COLLEGE, OXFORD. 1963

10. MOUNT OMEGA. 1963

11. RICH DEATH. 1962

12. LONGFORD CASTLE IN AN IMAGINARY SETTING. 1963

13. THE TOUCH OF DAY. 1963

14. THE SLANTED LIGHT : Side view. 1963

15. THE SLANTED LIGHT: Front view

16. AGAINST THE DAY: the bowl, enlarged. 1964

17 (opposite). AGAINST THE DAY: the whole glass

18. DRIVING WESTWARDS. 1964

19. BLAGDON, NORTHUMBERLAND. 1964

20. AND SUMMER AND WINTER: the bowl. 1965

21 (opposite). AND SUMMER AND WINTER: the whole glass. The title is continuous round the f

22. GLENALMOND. 1966

23. IDEA OF A CITY. 1966

24. FROM THE DEAD TO THE QUICK: front view. 1968

25. FROM THE DEAD TO THE QUICK : side view

26. MAGDALEN COLLEGE, OXFORD. 1966

27. FROCWARD CARSELBAR : an invented Vanbrugh house. 1966

28. THROUGH THE GATE OF A DREAM: side view. 1966

29. THROUGH THE GATE OF A DREAM: front view

30 (opposite). THE BANK OF ENGLAND: the Soane interior. 1967

31 (above). THE BANK OF ENGLAND ON THE CLIFF: an allegory. 1967

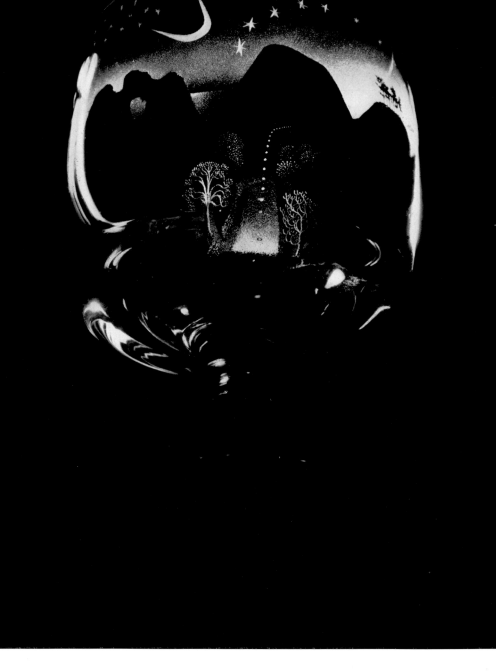

32. DORSET NIGHTFALL – WESSEX DAYBREAK. 1968

33 (opposite). A SEASONS CENTREPIECE: of glass and silver-gilt,
with revolving wings. 1968. The individual wings are illustrated overleaf

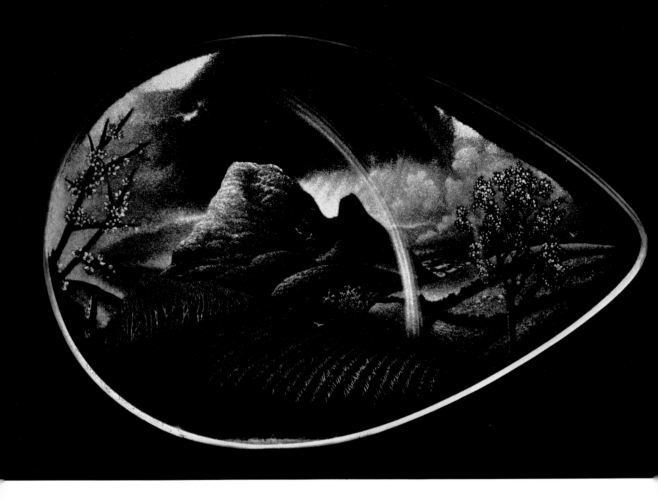

34. THE FOUR SEASONS: SPRING and SUMMER

35. THE FOUR SEASONS: AUTUMN and WINTER

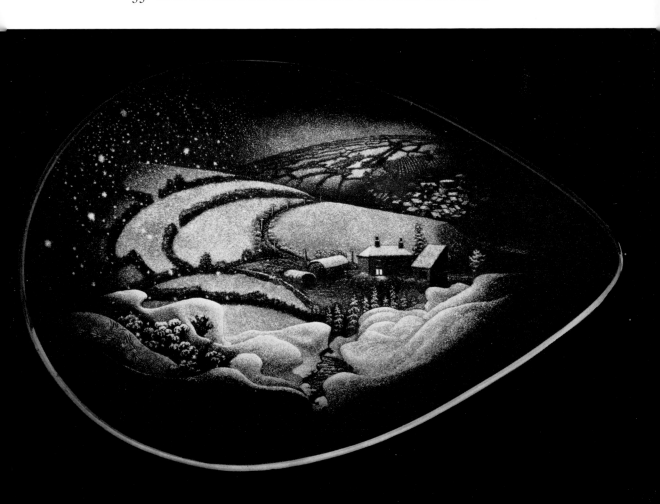

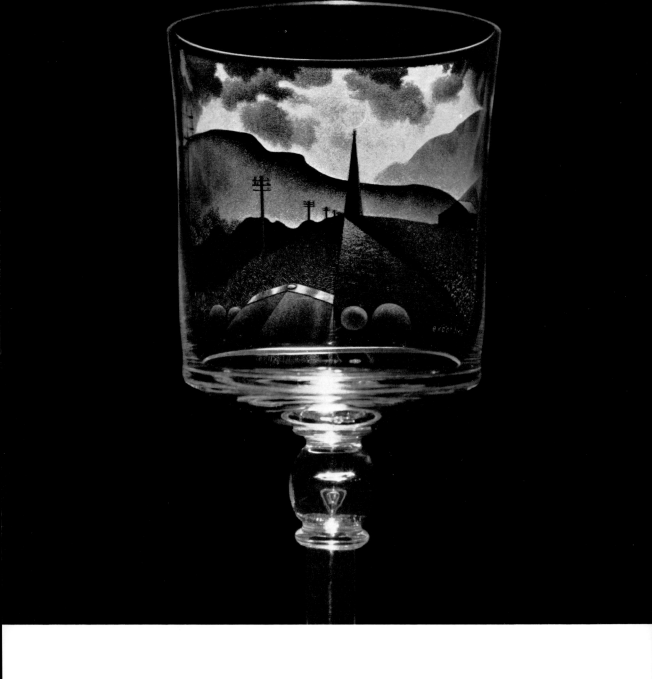

36. EXACT TIME: APPOINTED PLACE. 1968

37. EXACT TIME: APPOINTED PLACE: side view

38. THE FESTIVAL: for a Golden Wedding in 1968

39 (opposite). THE FESTIVAL: in its gilt-bronze frame

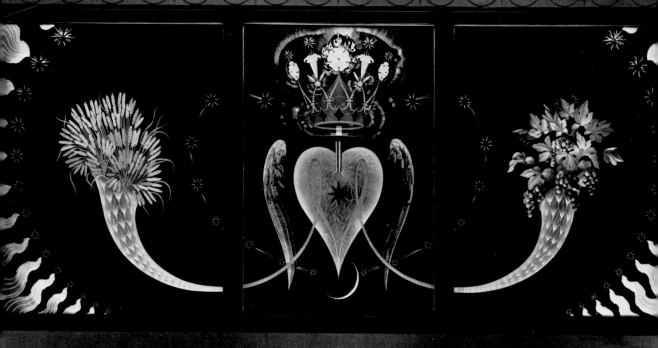

41. FROM THE RUINED TOWER. 1968

40 (opposite). REREDOS IN SHERBORNE ABBEY. 1969

42. VALSE TRISTE. 1969

43. CHI-RHO AT TWILIGHT. 1968

44. THE ENCOUNTER. 1969

45. THE ENCOUNTER: another view

46. HIGH NOON. 1968

47. MAN-SPATE. 1969

48. MOUNT OF OLIVES. 1969

49. MOUNT OF OLIVES: side view

50. THE SIX OF SUMMER. 1969

51. A SENSE OF SUMMER. 1969

52. THE AVENUE WATCHED. 1969

53. THE WISHED-FOR. 1969

54. FROM CASTLE TO AIRPORT: for Her Majesty The Queen. 1970

55. WELSH FARM. 1970

56. WET LANE TOWARDS EVENING. 1969

57 (opposite). WET LANE TOWARDS EVENING: another view

58. THE WHITE WATER. 1970

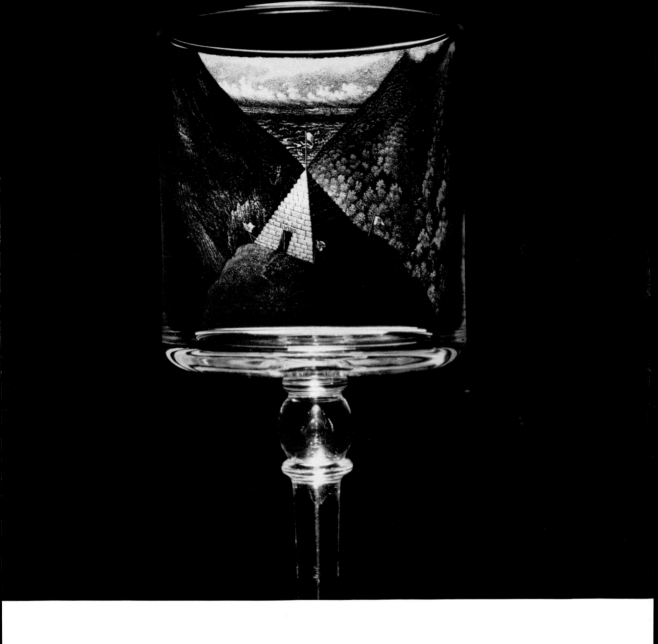

59. THE GAY MAUSOLEUM. 1970

60. THE TEMPLE OF NIGHT AND DAY. 1970

61. THE TEMPLE OF NIGHT AND DAY: another view

62. THE EVENING PLANE. 1970

63. THE EVENING PLANE: another view

WEMYSS CASTLE
FIFE

According to the proposal
of Sir John Vanbrugh
c. 1717

64. WEMYSS CASTLE: a window-pane showing a fictitious rebuilding by Vanbrugh. 1970

Thomas Alexander third Lord Hesketh

1950   OCTOBER 28   1971

65. EASTON NESTON: a window-pane. 1971

66. A KIND OF ALTARPIECE. 1971

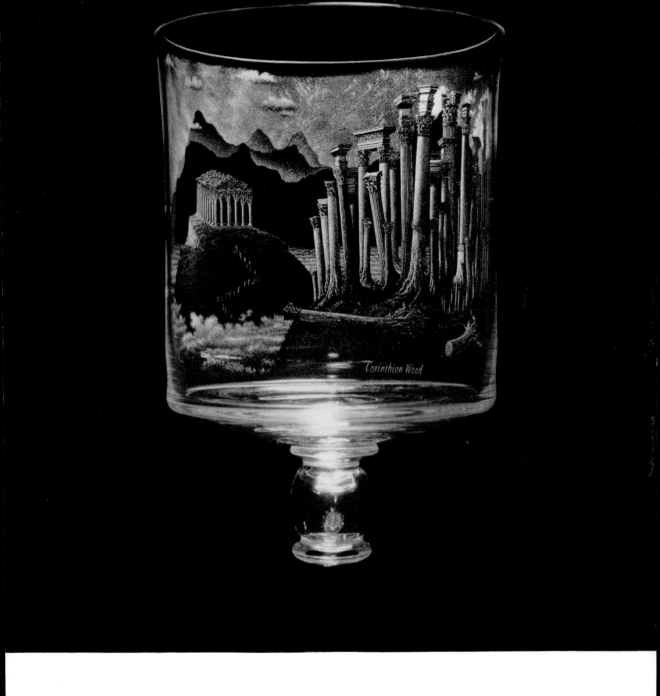

67. CORINTHIAN WOOD. See also frontispiece. 1971

68. A WINDOW TO EDWARD AND HELEN THOMAS: Eastbury, Berkshire. 1971

ERIC PRUE

1947 29 January 1972

69. STERNFIELD HOUSE, SUFFOLK: a window-pane. 1972

70. SPRING MOON. 1971

71. THE TUNNEL. 1972

72. IN THE LIGHT OF MODERN PROGRESS. 1972

73. THE LOST ORDER. 1972

74. THE GRASS CATHEDRAL. 1972

75. WAY OUT. 1971

76 and 77. ENTER. 1970

78. TRIPTYCH IN YEW WOOD. 1971

79. TRIPTYCH IN YEW WOOD: another view

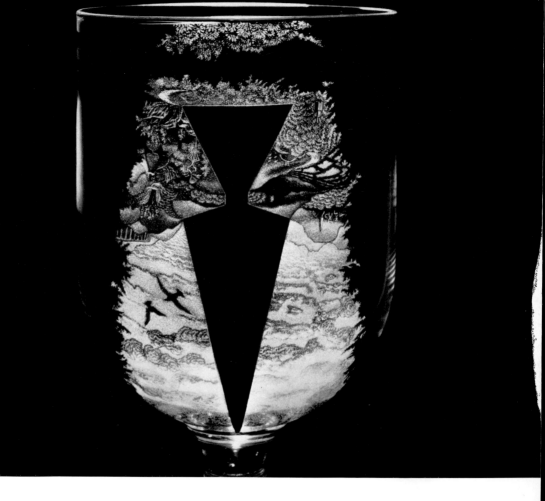

80. TERM